"It is the heart that makes
one great or small."
— MUHAMMAD ALI

MUHAMMAD ALI

BY CLAY LATIMER

The
Child's
World®

GRAPHIC DESIGN
Robert E. Bonaker / Graphic Design & Consulting Co.

PROJECT COORDINATOR
James R. Rothaus / James R. Rothaus & Associates

EDITORIAL DIRECTION
Elizabeth Sirimarco Budd

COVER PHOTO
Portrait of Muhammad Ali
©Michael Brennan/CORBIS

Library of Congress Cataloging-in-Publication Data
Latimer, Clay, 1952–
Muhammad Ali / by Clay Latimer.
p. cm.
Includes bibliographical references ( ) and index.
Summary: A simple biography of the legendary boxer,
Muhammad Ali, describing his accomplishments as a
fighter, as well as his impact on and contributions to society.
ISBN 1-56766-723-6 (lib. bdg. : alk. paper)

1. Ali, Muhammad, 1942– 2. Boxers (Sports) — United States
— Biography — Juvenile literature. [1. Ali, Muhammad, 1942–
2. Boxers (Sports) 3. Afro-Americans — Biography.] I. Title

GV1132.A44 L28 2000
796.83'092 — dc21   99-047617
[B]

Contents

The Start of Something Big

Cassius Clay couldn't believe his bad luck. He had ridden his new bicycle to a fair in his hometown of Louisville, Kentucky. He parked it carefully outside the fairgrounds. Then he and a friend wandered from booth to booth for hours. They stuffed themselves with popcorn and ice cream. They played games and enjoyed themselves. Finally, it was time to go home.

The boys went back to find their bicycles. But Cassius's shiny, red bike was gone! He looked all around him. It was nowhere to be seen. Cassius was stunned.

Someone told Cassius he could find a policeman in the basement of a nearby building. Cassius hurried down the stairs and into the Columbine Gym.

When he found the policeman, he demanded a search party to track down the thief of his missing bicycle. "I'm gonna whip him if I can find him!" threatened 12-year-old Cassius.

"Before you start fighting," the policeman told him, "you better learn how to fight."

Cassius looked around and realized where he was. Suddenly, he saw something that would change his life forever: a boxing ring.

Cassius forgot all about his bike. He asked the men at the gym if he could come back some time. He wanted to learn how to box. Cassius returned the very next day — and nearly every day after that for a long time to come. "I'll be the greatest fighter ever," he soon boasted to his friends.

CASSIUS CLAY AT AGE **12.** THE CAREER OF HISTORY'S GREATEST HEAVYWEIGHT BOXING CHAMPION BEGAN AFTER HIS BICYCLE WAS STOLEN IN **1954.**

©Michael Brennan/CORBIS

IN 1964, CASSIUS CLAY CHANGED HIS NAME TO MUHAMMAD ALI, BUT MANY PEOPLE SIMPLY CALL HIM "THE GREATEST."

Cassius later changed his name to Muhammad Ali. He became famous for his unmatched speed and skill in the boxing ring. Sports fans admired his courage. They also enjoyed his humor and **showmanship.** Muhammad Ali may be most famous for winning the **heavyweight** championship three times, something no boxer had ever done before.

But Ali's true greatness has come outside of the boxing ring. He has always stood up for what he believes. Today he is known for his bravery, his generosity, and his strength.

"I am the greatest," Ali often said, "of all time."

The Courier Journal, Louisville, Kentucky

ALI HAS NOT BOXED SINCE **1981,** BUT HE STILL LOVES TO MEET HIS FANS AND SIGN AUTOGRAPHS.

The Early Rounds

In the beginning, Cassius was just like many other boys in Louisville, Kentucky. He was born on January 17, 1942. His mother, Odessa, was quiet and religious. She was her son's role model. His father, Cassius Clay Sr., was fiery and artistic. He gave Cassius his courage and strength. Cassius also had a younger brother named Rudy.

The Clay family lived in a comfortable home in a nice neighborhood. Cassius never worried about violence, gangs, or other big-city problems. Still, black people and white people in Louisville lived in separate worlds. Like many southern cities at the time, Louisville had **segregation** laws. What did these laws do? They kept black people and white people apart.

African Americans in Kentucky could not eat in the same restaurants as white people. They could not sit with whites at a theater or ball game. Black children often could not attend the same schools or share classrooms with white children.

African Americans faced other kinds of **discrimination,** too. They had a difficult time finding good jobs. Many were stuck in jobs that did not pay well. White people even tried to keep blacks from voting in elections.

Such treatment angered Cassius's father. He believed he could have been an artist in an **integrated** world. Instead, he painted signs for a living.

Cassius Jr. shared his father's anger. At an early age, he dreamed of helping African Americans lead better lives. "I always felt I was born to do something for my people," he later remembered. "I'd look out of my house at two in the morning . . . I'd look at the stars and wait for a voice, but I never heard nothing."

Cassius discovered boxing instead. When boxing made him famous, he used his fame to fight **racism** and poverty.

The Courier Journal, Louisville, Kentucky

CASSIUS AND HIS PARENTS, ODESSA AND CASSIUS SR., SHOW
OFF A PAINTING OF THE YOUNG CHAMP IN THE RING.

CASSIUS LOVED TO BOX. HE SPENT ALL HIS FREE TIME PRACTICING TO BE THE BEST. ONE DAY, HE WOULD BE A CHAMPION.

Boxing became Cassius's passion. It was the most important thing in his life. He knew it would take work to become a champion. Day after day, month after month, he worked to get stronger. He practiced his **footwork.** He practiced punching. He raced alongside the school bus, punching an imaginary opponent. Sometimes he even raced the horses that trained at nearby Churchill Downs, the famous racetrack of the Kentucky Derby.

Cassius was always the first to arrive at the gym and the last to leave. He thought about boxing all the time, even when he wasn't at the gym. He wanted to be stronger and faster than any boxer had ever been.

Training wasn't easy, and he didn't always like it. Still, Cassius made himself work even when he didn't want to. "Don't quit," he would tell himself. "Suffer now and live the rest of your life as a champion."

By the time he was 16 years old, Cassius weighed 170 pounds. He stood 6 feet tall. By age 18, he had won the national Golden Gloves **title,** an important honor in the sport of boxing. In 1960, Cassius graduated from Central High School. That summer, he won a gold medal in the Olympics. Cassius Clay was on his way to a professional boxing career.

CASSIUS'S FAMILY CONGRATULATES HIM AFTER HE RETURNS FROM THE 1960 OLYMPICS.

The Courier Journal, Louisville, Kentucky

The Greatest

The sports world has many famous celebrities, but Cassius Clay was one of the first. He enjoyed watching himself on television. Seeing his name in newspapers thrilled him. He loved hearing people talk about him.

Cassius liked to talk about himself even more. He bragged that he was the smartest champ, the prettiest champ, the fastest champ, and of course, the greatest champ. Sometimes he even bragged about himself with poems.

Cassius's poetry summed up his personality. It could be silly, playful, or cruel. The poems attracted attention, and Cassius loved attention — especially before a fight. He even used his poetry to predict the end of fights. "They all fall in the **round** I call," Cassius claimed. Many fights did end in the round that Cassius predicted. He was correct in 13 of his first 17 fights as a **professional** boxer!

Cassius was a star in the ring. His movements were graceful and smooth. He even got on his toes and danced around his opponents.

Boxing experts were amazed. They had never seen such a big man move so quickly. Cassius would dangle his fists at his waist. This left his head unprotected. Most boxers would never do such a thing. But Cassius was much quicker than other boxers. Just when an opponent was about to land a punch, Cassius would move his head out of the way.

Cassius won his first 19 fights as a professional. Then he was ready to meet a boxer named Sonny Liston. Liston was the heavyweight champion. He terrified opponents with his brutal power. Everyone was afraid of Liston — except Cassius Clay. Liston agreed to defend his title against Cassius on February 25, 1964.

©Bettmann/CORBIS

A FRIEND HAD TO HOLD BACK AN ANGRY CASSIUS CLAY AFTER HE TRIED TO LUNGE AT SONNY LISTON DURING THE WEIGH-IN. OFFICIALS FINED CASSIUS $2,500 FOR HIS BEHAVIOR.

Sports fans weren't so sure that Cassius could win. Liston himself wasn't worried. "I don't know what I'm training for," he said. "This kid ain't gonna last one round."

At the **weigh-in,** Cassius seemed to lose his mind. He screamed wildly at Liston. His blood pressure shot to dangerous levels. Was Cassius Clay crazy?

"I don't think this kid's all there," Liston grumbled.

But something strange happened. An hour or two later, Cassius's blood pressure was almost normal. He was perfectly calm. His strange antics had all been an act.

"Liston is a bully, and a bully is scared of a crazy man," Cassius said. "Now Liston thinks I'm crazy. I got him worried."

Before the fight, Cassius's assistant told him to "float like a butterfly and sting like a bee." He did just that. Liston couldn't hit Cassius because he couldn't catch him. Liston couldn't stop Cassius's punches because he didn't see them coming. Cassius Clay was just too fast.

Cassius danced around the ring. Liston just stumbled.

In the 3rd round, Cassius cut Liston's cheek. In the 4th round, Cassius continued to do everything right. But near the end of that round, his eyes began to sting.

"I can't see," Cassius yelled. "My eyes, my eyes! Cut the gloves off. We're going home."

Cassius's manager calmed him down. He washed Cassius's eyes and sent him back into the ring.

In the 7th round, Cassius was at his best. Liston looked tired and beaten. Liston quit before the round was over. He said he had an injured shoulder.

Cassius Clay went wild. He howled and jumped around the ring. "I shook up the world," he screamed. "I'm the greatest thing that ever lived. I don't have a mark on my face, and I upset Sonny Liston, and I just turned 22 years old."

On May 25, 1965, Cassius met Liston again. This time, the champ knocked out Liston in the very first round.

No one knew for sure if he could do it, but Cassius Clay won his first fight against Liston in the 7th round. The two heavyweights met again in May 1965. This time, Cassius knocked out Liston in the first minute of the match.

The Toughest Fight

Cassius Clay shocked the world when he took the heavyweight title away from Sonny Liston. After the fight, he shocked the world again. He told reporters that he was a member of a group called the **Nation of Islam.**

The Nation of Islam is a smaller group within the religion of **Islam.** Members of the Nation of Islam are called Black **Muslims.** They believe that African Americans would be better off living in a separate society, away from whites. They feel it is the only way that black people will ever have equal rights.

Cassius first heard about the Nation of Islam at a boxing tournament in 1959. Two years later, he went to a meeting of the Black Muslims. "After that, my life changed," he once said.

Malcolm X was a leader of the Nation of Islam. Before the Liston fight, he often visited Cassius. There were rumors that Cassius had joined the group. But the public did not know for sure until after the fight. Soon, another important leader, Elijah Muhammad, gave Cassius a new name: Muhammad Ali. (Muhammad is the name of an important Muslim prophet. Many Muslims are named in his honor.)

Most Americans didn't like Ali's decision to join the Nation of Islam. But Ali didn't like segregation and racism. It angered him that the color of his skin limited his freedom. He had won an Olympic gold medal for the United States. He was the heavyweight champion of the world. Yet he still could not eat in some Louisville restaurants.

Ali had fought in the boxing ring and won. Now he wanted to fight racism, too. He believed that joining the Nation of Islam was one way to do it.

MUHAMMAD ALI GIVES A SPEECH AT
A NATION OF ISLAM MEETING.

At first, both white people and African Americans attacked Ali. An ex-heavyweight champion named Floyd Patterson was especially angry. Patterson was an African American, too. "I have nothing but contempt for the Black Muslims and that for which they stand," Patterson said. "Cassius Clay must be beaten and the Black Muslims' **scourge** removed from boxing."

Ali agreed to defend his title against Patterson on November 22, 1965. It was more than a fight to him. It was war.

In the 1st round, Ali danced around Patterson without throwing a single punch. In the 2nd round, Ali teased Patterson. Just before Patterson was ready to quit, Ali eased up just enough to keep Patterson going. The cruel fight ended when Patterson finally collapsed in the 12th round.

Ali's greatest fight was still to come, but it would take place outside the ring. The United States first entered the **Vietnam War** in 1964. Many Americans believed their country should not have been involved. During the war, many young American men were **drafted** into the **armed forces.** When people are drafted, it is illegal for them to refuse to join the military without a very good reason. In 1967, Ali was drafted, but he refused to join the armed forces. He said he could not participate in a war because it was against his strong religious beliefs.

Ali appeared for his **induction** on April 28, 1967. An officer called his name and told Ali to stand up. Ali refused. His name was called twice more. Ali refused twice more. The officer warned Ali that he was committing a crime. He told Ali he could be punished. Ali still refused to step forward.

Finally, Ali was arrested. He spent the next 10 days in jail. Some people said Ali simply did not want to go to war. They did not believe that his beliefs were really so strong. The boxing world also turned its back on him. His heavyweight title was taken away. Muhammad Ali, The Greatest, was no longer allowed to box in the United States.

Library of Congress

MUHAMMAD ALI AND HIS LAWYER PREPARE TO GO TO TRIAL. AFTER HE REFUSED
TO ENTER THE ARMY, ALI LOST HIS HEAVYWEIGHT TITLE. HE DID NOT FIGHT IN
THE UNITED STATES FOR MORE THAN THREE YEARS.

Ali's trial took place in June of 1967. An all-white jury found him guilty. He was **sentenced** to five years in prison and fined $10,000. He decided to **appeal** the ruling. That meant he would ask a more important court to change the decision.

In the meantime, Ali continued to attend Nation of Islam meetings. He studied the teachings of Elijah Muhammad. He traveled around the country to meet with other Black Muslims. He spoke to people at Muslim **mosques** and in Christian churches. He also spoke to students on college campuses.

In August, Ali married Belinda Boyd. She was only 17 years old. Belinda shared Ali's religious beliefs. She was a Black Muslim, too. In their years together, they had four children.

Ali could not box for three-and-a-half years. During that time, the United States was slowly turning against the war. Many people began to believe that Ali was sincere. With more public support, Ali was able to box again. Muhammad Ali returned to the ring on October 26, 1970. His opponent was Jerry Quarry. Ali won in just three rounds.

Ali won a much more important fight on June 28, 1971. The Supreme Court decided that Muhammad Ali was not guilty of draft **evasion.** The judges believed that his faith really did stop him from going to war.

Ali would not have to go to jail, nor would he have to pay the $10,000 fine. Everyone expected Ali to celebrate wildly, and even to brag about his victory. That was not the case. "I've done my celebrating already," Ali said. "I said a prayer to **Allah.**"

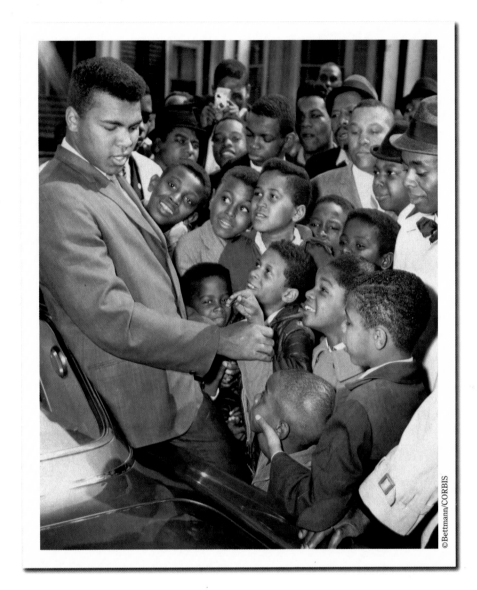

©Bettmann/CORBIS

DURING THE THREE YEARS IN WHICH ALI COULD NOT BOX, HE TRAVELED AROUND THE COUNTRY MEETING OTHER MEMBERS OF THE NATION OF ISLAM. IN BOSTON, YOUNG MEMBERS OF THE TEMPLE ISLAM GATHERED TO MEET THE CHAMP AFTER HE GAVE A SPEECH.

The Comeback

Ali could not box professionally for more than three years. Now that he was 29 years old, some people wondered if he was still the world's best boxer. Had sports fans already seen him at his best? Even Ali wondered if he was still "The Greatest."

"I was better when I was young," he said. "I had my speed when I was young. I was faster on my legs, and my hands were faster."

During Ali's long break from boxing, there was a tournament to determine who the new heavyweight champion would be. The winner's name was Joe Frazier.

Once Ali could return to the ring, he agreed to fight Frazier. Frazier was unbeaten, but so was Ali. Never before had an unbeaten heavyweight champion fought an unbeaten ex-champ. It was billed as "The Fight of the Century."

It was March 8, 1971. Twenty-five thousand fans crammed into New York City's Madison Square Garden to see the fight. About 300 million more people watched the fight on television.

Ali and Frazier climbed into the ring. The air practically crackled with excitement. The very first seconds of the fight were thrilling. In the same instant, Frazier and Ali both landed punches. This would be one incredible match.

Ali won the first two rounds, but he wasn't as fast as he once was. Frazier got the better of Ali in the next rounds. By the 8th round, it even looked as if Ali was giving up.

Things changed in the 9th round. Ali buried Frazier in a stream of lightning-fast punches. For the first time, Frazier backed away. Ali was fighting for his life — and his pride.

©Bettmann/CORBIS

STRAPPING ON HIS CHAMPIONSHIP BELT AT A
PRE-FIGHT PHYSICAL, ALI DECLARED, "JOE
FRAZIER DOESN'T HAVE THE REAL BELT. HOW
CAN YOU HAVE TWO CHAMPIONS?"

©Bettmann/CORBIS

FRAZIER LANDS A NASTY LEFT HOOK DURING "THE FIGHT OF THE CENTURY" ON MARCH 8, 1971.

In the 11th round, Frazier nearly knocked out Ali. But somehow, Ali managed to stay on his feet. Frazier landed another hard punch. Ali fell into the ropes. The bell rang to end the round.

Just 20 seconds into the last round, Frazier threw the most famous punch in boxing history. It knocked Ali flat on his back. "I looked up, and I was on the floor," Ali said.

Ali got up immediately. But it was too late. Frazier had won.

Ali and Frazier both ended up in the hospital. Doctors treated Ali's swollen jaw, and then he went home. Frazier's injuries were more severe. He was in and out of the hospital for two weeks.

Ali vowed he would fight for the title again. He won his next 10 fights. Fans believed he was on his way back. But then he lost to Ken Norton on March 31, 1973. Ali's jaw was broken, but he didn't give up. Later that year, he beat Norton in a rematch. In the meantime, Frazier lost his title to George Foreman.

Ali defeated Frazier on January 28, 1974. Now it was time to meet George Foreman. The fight would take place in Zaire, Africa. People called it "The Rumble in the Jungle."

Ali and Foreman departed for Africa in September 1974, 15 days before their fight. A week later, Foreman suffered a cut above his right eye during training. The fight was rescheduled for October 30. Ali and Foreman were in Zaire for a total of 44 days.

The people of Zaire loved Muhammad Ali. He joked with old men. He hugged children. He chatted with families. He even did magic tricks. Nearly everyone in Zaire was pulling for Ali. Even so, few sports fans believed he would win. People called Foreman the unbeatable champion.

Once again, Ali fooled everybody.

In the 2nd round, Ali led Foreman to the edge of the ring. Then he spread his feet wide and leaned on the ropes. Foreman landed one powerful punch after another.

Ali covered his head with his arms and took the punishment. He hardly threw any punches at all. What was Ali thinking?

Of course, Ali had a plan. He wanted Foreman to get tired. Then, when Foreman ran out of energy, he would attack. Ali even had a name for this strategy: Rope-a-Dope.

Foreman kept flailing away, round after round. It was a hot, sticky night. Foreman grew more and more tired.

Foreman hadn't trained for a long fight. He thought he would beat Ali in the early rounds. But Ali would not fall. In the 8th round, Ali knocked Foreman down with a flurry of punches. Foreman couldn't get back up in time.

It was 10 years after he had beaten Sonny Liston. It was seven years after he had been stripped of his title. Ali had finally regained the heavyweight title.

Ali's next big fight took place on October 1, 1975. It was against Joe Frazier. This time, they traveled to the city of Manila in the Philippines. People called the fight the "Thrilla [thriller] in Manila."

Ali dominated the early rounds. Frazier controlled the middle rounds. With four rounds to go, Ali was in trouble. But he reached deep into himself for courage. He took over in the 13th round. By the 14th round, Frazier's eyes were nearly swollen shut. When the bell rang for the 15th round, Frazier's manager threw in the towel. Ali was the winner.

After beating Frazier, Ali won his next six fights. He was ready for an easy opponent. He scheduled a fight against a young boxer named Leon Spinks.

Spinks had fought only seven times as a professional. Ali thought he would be easy to beat. He did not train as hard as he could have.

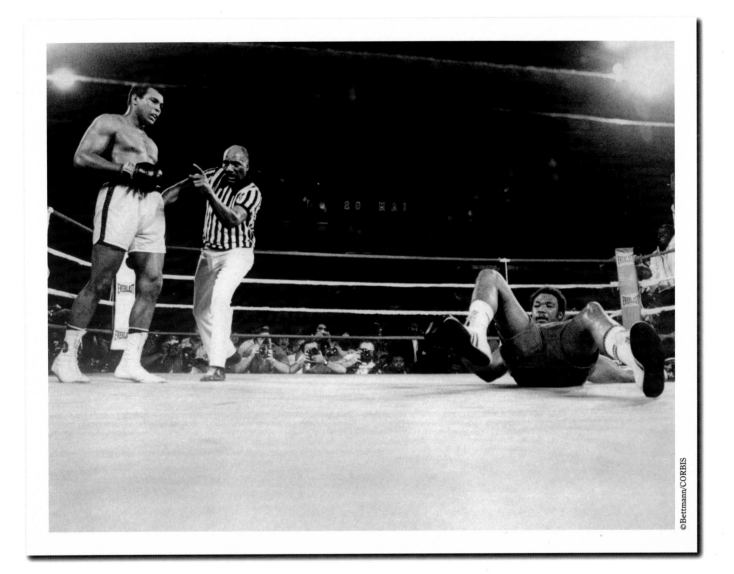

©Bettmann/CORBIS

GEORGE FOREMAN LOOKS UP FROM THE RING AFTER MUHAMMAD ALI KNOCKS HIM DOWN IN THE 8TH ROUND OF "THE RUMBLE IN THE JUNGLE."

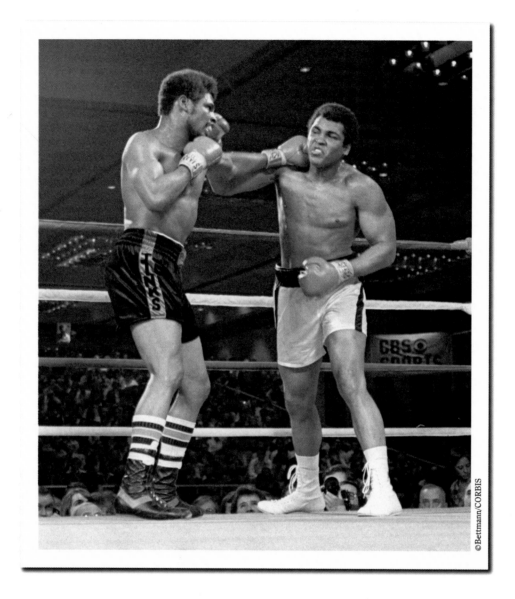

SPINKS BEAT ALI IN THEIR FEBRUARY 1978 MATCH-UP. FANS WONDERED IF ALI WOULD EVER BE THE HEAVYWEIGHT CHAMP AGAIN. IN A REMATCH LATER THAT YEAR, HE PROVED HE WAS STILL THE GREATEST. HE BECAME THE FIRST BOXER TO WIN THE HEAVYWEIGHT TITLE THREE TIMES.

But on February 15, 1978, Spinks surprised Ali — and boxing fans around the world. In the 15th round, Spinks was the winner — and the new heavyweight champion.

Ali made sure he was ready for a rematch against Spinks. He was in fantastic shape, and he won the fight. On September 15, 1978, Ali became the first boxer to win the heavyweight title three times.

Ali was ready to stop fighting. On June 27, 1979, he announced his plan to retire. A little more than one year later, he agreed to fight Larry Holmes for the title. Ali still loved attention, and the winner would get $8 million. Ali couldn't say no.

The fight took place in Las Vegas on October 2, 1980. For 10 horrible rounds, Holmes punished Ali. Several times,

Holmes looked at the referee, hoping he would stop the fight. After 10 rounds, he finally did. Ali spent the next two days in a hospital.

Ali wasn't finished. He agreed to fight Trevor Berbick. It was clear in the first minutes of the fight that Ali didn't belong in a ring anymore. Ali lost the fight in 10 rounds and then retired for good.

"Father Time caught up with me," Ali said after the fight. "I'm finished."

MUHAMMAD ALI DANCES AROUND THE RING DURING HIS WORKOUT SESSION AT CAESAR'S PALACE IN LAS VEGAS, NEVADA. ALI WAS PREPARING FOR HIS TITLE FIGHT WITH LARRY HOLMES.

Reuters/Andy Clark/Archive Photos

MUHAMMAD ALI WAS DIAGNOSED WITH PARKINSON'S DISEASE IN 1984. WHEN HE APPEARED AT THE OPENING CEREMONIES OF THE 1996 OLYMPICS, HIS FANS HADN'T SEEN HIM FOR MANY YEARS. HE SEEMED VERY DIFFERENT FROM THE SWIFT, GRACEFUL CHAMP THEY REMEMBERED. BUT TO MANY, HE WAS STILL THE GREATEST.

The Most Famous Man in the World

In 1996, the world watched the opening ceremonies of the Summer Olympics. Boxer Evander Holyfield brought the Olympic torch into the stadium. He handed it off to an American swimmer named Janet Evans. She circled the track and ran up a ramp toward the cauldron.

Then it happened. Muhammad Ali stepped into the stadium and into the spotlight. He took the flame from Evans. With 300 million people watching, he lit the flame to signal the start of the Olympic Games. The emotion of the moment brought tears of joy to many people.

Other people were saddened. Ali looked very different from the champion people remembered. His arms trembled as he lit the flame. He didn't look like the self-confident boxer he once was. What had happened to the smartest, most graceful heavyweight champ in history?

The years following his retirement had been difficult for Ali. He missed boxing. He had money problems. His third marriage was failing. But his biggest problem was poor health.

In 1984, doctors determined that Ali had **Parkinson's disease.** People with this disease have **tremors,** poor balance, and trouble speaking. Ali experiences all of these difficulties.

Although Ali has trouble talking, his mind is still sharp. The illness is not life threatening. In fact, his friends say Ali has developed a new sense of peace. He still has his deep religious beliefs. Over time, Ali began to dislike some of the beliefs of the Nation of Islam. He believed that such ideas drove people from different races further apart. Today he practices a different form of Islam. He also has a happy relationship with his fourth wife, Lonnie. They were married in 1986.

Muhammad Ali spends much of his time raising money to help people. He has raised money to pay for research to fight Parkinson's disease. He raises money to feed the hungry around the world. He also speaks out to audiences around the country against youth violence and racism.

Ali helps people all over the world. He has traveled to Africa, Asia, and Latin America to bring food and money to the poor. In 1990, he went to Iraq during the Gulf War. His visit with Iraqi leader Saddam Hussein helped bring about the release of American hostages. He also traveled to war-torn Bosnia to call for peace.

Muhammad Ali has given sports fans a wealth of memories. At 18 years old, he won an Olympic gold medal. By the time he was 22, he was the heavyweight champion of the world.

The young man named Cassius Clay said he could beat Sonny Liston, and he did. Years later, now a world-famous boxer, Muhammad Ali beat George Foreman when people said it was impossible. In 1978, he became the first boxer to win the heavyweight title three times.

Muhammad Ali did all these things and more. His skill, speed, and bravery made him the greatest boxer of all time. His compassion and faith have made him "The Greatest" outside of the boxing ring, too. Muhammad Ali has always believed in himself. He works hard. And he never gives up, no matter how hard the fight.

The Courier Journal, Louisville, Kentucky

ALI'S WIFE LONNIE PLAYFULLY PINCHES HIS CHEEK. THE COUPLE MARRIED IN 1986.

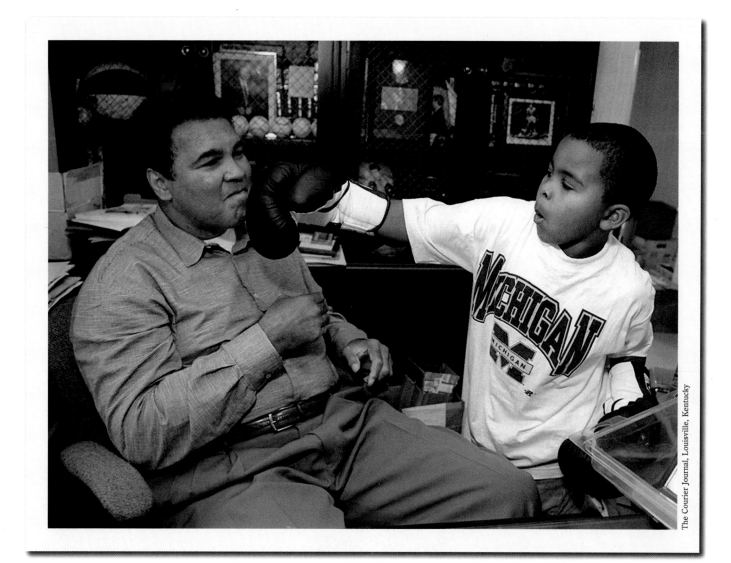

The Courier Journal, Louisville, Kentucky

ALI'S SON ASAAD GIVES HIS FATHER A PLAYFUL PUNCH. NOW THAT THE CHAMP
HAS RETIRED FROM BOXING, HE HAS MORE TIME TO SPEND WITH HIS FAMILY.

Timeline

1942	Cassius Clay is born in Louisville, Kentucky, on January 17.
1954	Cassius learns to box at the Columbine Gym in Louisville.
1959	Cassius learns about the Nation of Islam.
1960	Cassius graduates from Central High School in Louisville. He wins an Olympic gold medal in the light-heavyweight division. He also wins his first professional fight.
1964	Cassius wins the heavyweight title by beating Sonny Liston. After the fight, he announces that he is a member of the Nation of Islam. He changes his name to Muhammad Ali.
1965	Ali successfully defends his heavyweight title against Sonny Liston with a knockout in the 1st round.
1967	Ali refuses to join the armed forces because of his religious beliefs. An all-white jury convicts him of avoiding the draft. The judge gives him the maximum sentence: five years in jail and a $10,000 fine. Ali appeals the verdict. He loses his championship title and cannot box in the United States.
1970	Ali returns to the boxing ring. He beats Jerry Quarry and Oscar Bonavena in his first two fights in more than three years.
1971	The Supreme Court reverses Ali's conviction. Ali loses to Joe Frazier in a heavyweight championship fight. The battle is called "The Fight of the Century."
1974	Muhammad Ali beats Joe Frazier and then George Foreman. He is the heavyweight champion of the world for the second time.
1978	Ali loses the heavyweight title to Leon Spinks on February 15. He wins it back on September 15 and becomes the first three-time heavyweight champ.
1979	Ali announces his retirement.
1980	Ali returns to the ring for a fight against Larry Holmes. Referees stop the fight after 10 rounds, and Holmes is the winner. Ali spends two days in the hospital.
1981	Ali fights the last match of his career. He retires from boxing for good.
1984	Ali learns that he has Parkinson's disease.
1990	Ali is elected to the Boxing Hall of Fame.
1996	Ali lights the torch at the opening ceremony of the Summer Olympics.
1997	Ali testifies before the U.S. Congress to ask for increased funding to find a cure for Parkinson's disease.

Glossary

African Americans (AF-rih-kun uh-MAYR-ih-kunz)
African Americans are Americans whose ancestors came from the African continent. Muhammad Ali is an African American.

Allah (AH-luh)
Allah is the Muslim word for God. Muslims pray to Allah.

appeal (UH-peel)
When people appeal a court's decision, they ask a more powerful court to change the decision. Muhammad Ali appealed his conviction for refusing to join the armed forces after he was drafted.

armed forces (ARMD FOR-sez)
The armed forces are groups of soldiers that protect a nation. In the United States, the armed forces are the Army, the Navy, the Air Force, and the Marine Corps.

discrimination (dis-krim-ih-NAY-shun)
Discrimination is unfair treatment of people (such as preventing them from getting jobs or going to school) because they are different. African Americans have suffered discrimination by whites.

drafted (DRAF-ted)
If a young man is drafted, he has been selected to join the armed services. Muhammad Ali was drafted in 1967.

evasion (ee-VAY-zhen)
Evasion is an action that a person takes to avoid doing something. Muhammad Ali was accused of draft evasion.

footwork (FOOT-werk)
Footwork is the way in which boxers move their feet. Boxers must move around the ring quickly to defend themselves and to get into position to throw punches.

heavyweight (HEH-vee-wayt)
A heavyweight is a boxer who weighs more than 200 pounds. Boxers are divided into groups by their weight, and the heavyweights are the biggest fighters of all.

induction (in-DUK-shun)
An induction is a meeting in which a person is admitted to an organization. Muhammad Ali went to his induction into the armed forces, but he refused to join the miltary.

integrated (IN-tuh-gray-ted)
If something is integrated, it can be used equally by all races. Cassius Clay Sr. believed his life would have been different if Louisville had been integrated.

Islam (IZ-lahm)
Islam is a religion based on the teachings of a prophet named Muhammad. Muhammad Ali is a follower of Islam.

mosques (MOSKS)
Mosques are Muslim places of worship, similar to churches. Muhammad Ali visits mosques all over the world.

Muslims (MUZ-limz)
Muslims are people who follow the religion of Islam. Muhammad Ali is a Muslim.

Glossary

Nation of Islam (NAY-shun OF IZ-lahm)
The Nation of Islam is a smaller group within the religion of Islam. Members of the Nation of Islam are called Black Muslims.

Parkinson's disease (PAR-kin-sunz dih-ZEEZ)
Parkinson's disease is an illness that causes tremors and muscle weakness. Muhammad Ali suffers from Parkinson's disease.

professional (proh-FESH-uh-nul)
A professional is a person who gets paid to do something. Muhammad Ali was a professional boxer.

racism (RAY-sih-zim)
Racism is a negative feeling or opinion about people because of their race. Racism can be committed by individuals, large groups, or governments.

round (ROUND)
A round is part of a boxing match. A match has 12 to 15 rounds, and boxers take a short break between rounds.

scourge (SKERJ)
A scourge is something that causes trouble or misfortune. Boxer Floyd Patterson believed that Muhammad Ali's faith was a scourge on boxing.

segregation (seg-rih-GAY-shun)
Segregation is a situation in which actions and laws separate people from one another. Blacks and whites were segregated in the South for many years.

sentenced (SEN-tensd)
When people are sentenced, they receive punishment for a crime, such as a period of time in jail. A judge sentences people after they are convicted of a crime.

showmanship (SHO-man-ship)
Showmanship is the ability to entertain people. Muhammad Ali is famous for his sense of humor and his showmanship.

title (TY-tull)
A title is a first-place position in a championship. Muhammad Ali won the heavyweight boxing title three times.

tremors (TREM-urz)
Tremors are shaking or trembling movements that a person cannot stop. People with Parkinson's disease often have tremors.

Vietnam War (vee-et-NAHM WAR)
The Vietnam War was fought between southern and northern Vietnam to gain control of the entire country. Muhammad Ali refused to fight in the Vietnam War because of his religious beliefs.

weigh-in (WAY-in)
A weigh-in happens before a boxing match. Officials weigh both boxers and check to see if they are healthy.

Index

Further Information

Books

Bacho, Peter. *Boxing in Black and White: A History of the Great Heavyweight Fights.* New York: Henry Holt, 1999.

Cassidy, Robert. *Muhammad Ali: The Greatest of All Time.* Lincolnwood, IL: Publications International Ltd., 1999.

Knapp, Ron. *Top 10 Heavyweight Boxers* (Sports Top 10). Springfield, NJ: Enslow Publishers, 1997.

Sandelson, Robert. *Combat Sports* (Olympic Sports). New York: Crestwood House, 1991.

Web Sites

Read articles about and view pictures of Muhammad Ali from the *Louisville Courier-Journal,* the newspaper from his hometown (this site also includes some of Ali's famous poems): **http://www.courier-journal.com/ali/**

Learn about Muhammad Ali's trip to Indonesia to fight racism and poverty: **http://www.vitapro.com/palbum.htm**

Ali speaks out against racism: **http://xenocide.nando.net/newsroom/magazine/thirdrave/dec696/stars/1206mu.html**

Learn more about boxing at the International Boxing Hall of Fame Web site: **http://www.ibhof.com/ibhfhome.htm**

Listen to an interview with Muhammad Ali: **http://www.npr.org/ramfiles/me/19981106.me.15.ram**